INCREDIBLE STEPS TO DRAWING

Activity Guide

ACTIVIBOOKS FOR KIDS

activibooks for kids

Coloring, Drawing & Activity Books For Children

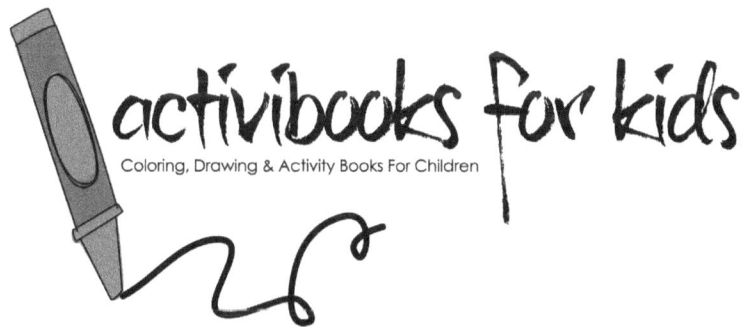

1
2
3
4
5
6

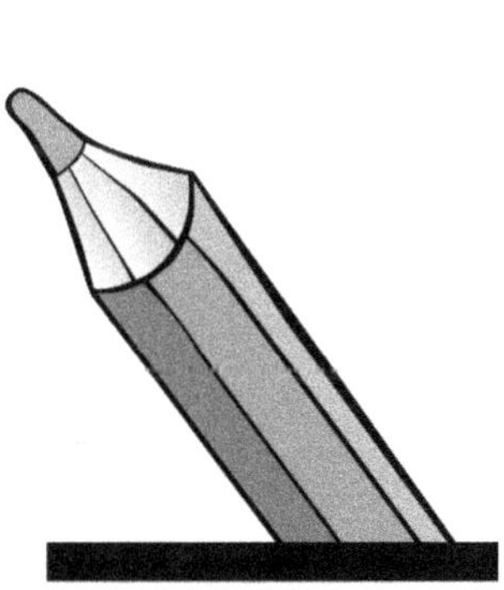

1
2
3
4
5
6

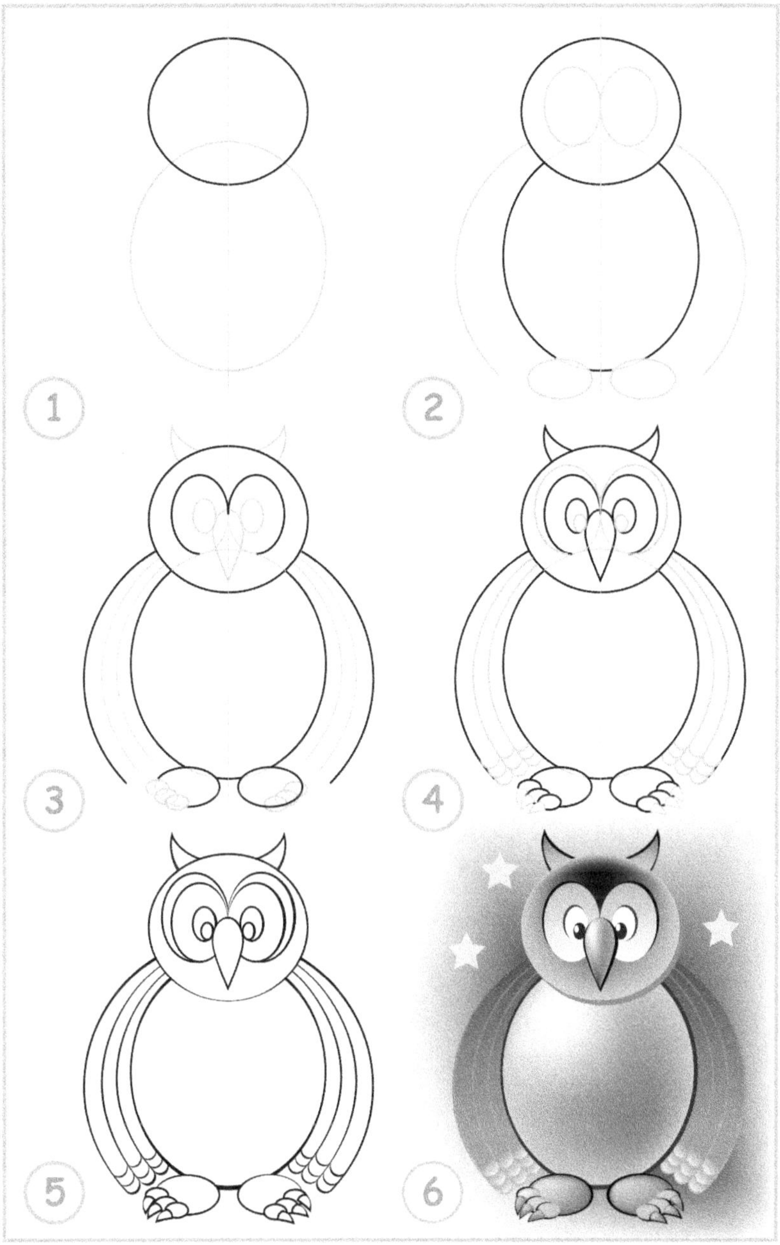
1
2
3
4
5
6

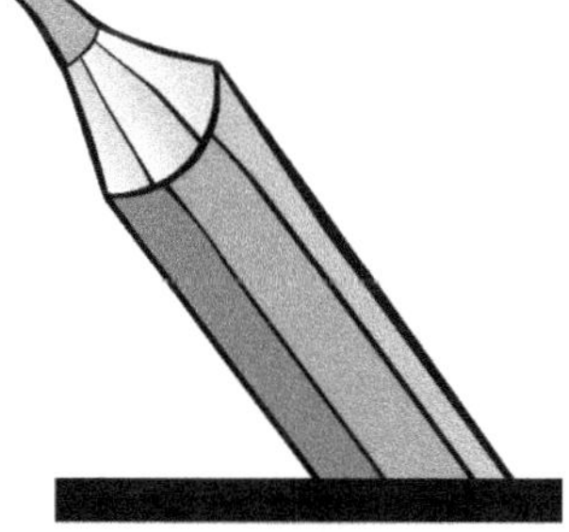

1
2
3
4
5
6

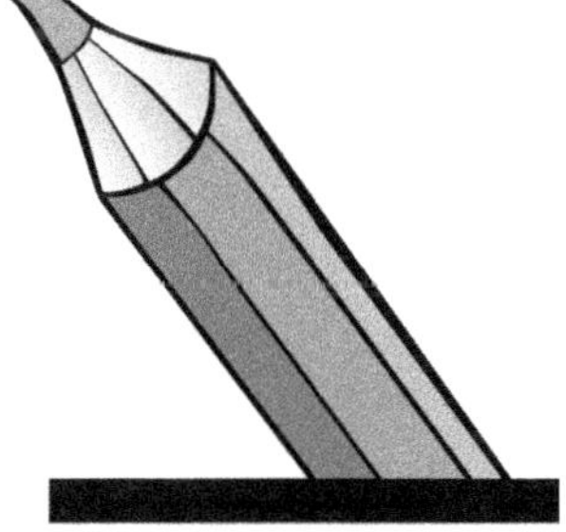

1
2
3
4
5
6

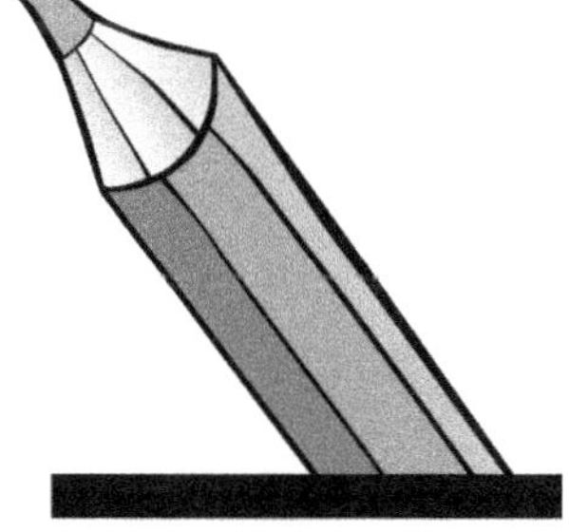

1
2
3
4
5
6

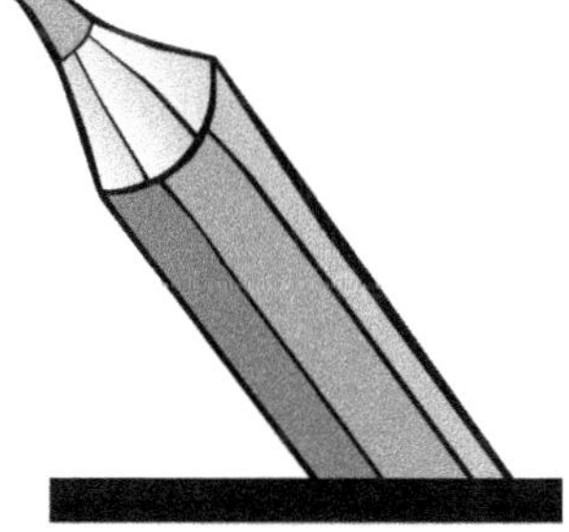

1
2
3
4
5
6

1
2
3
4
5
6

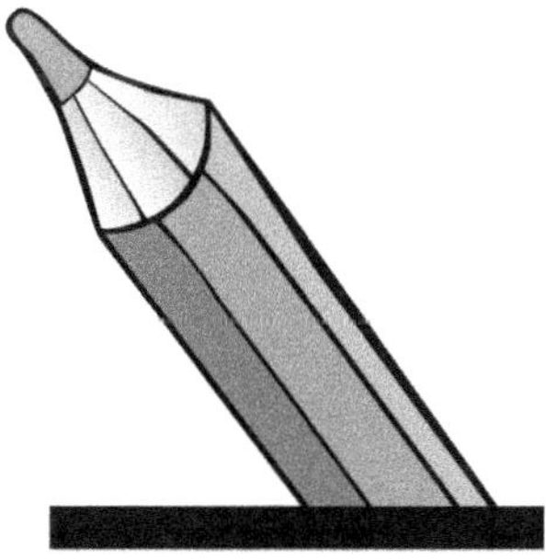

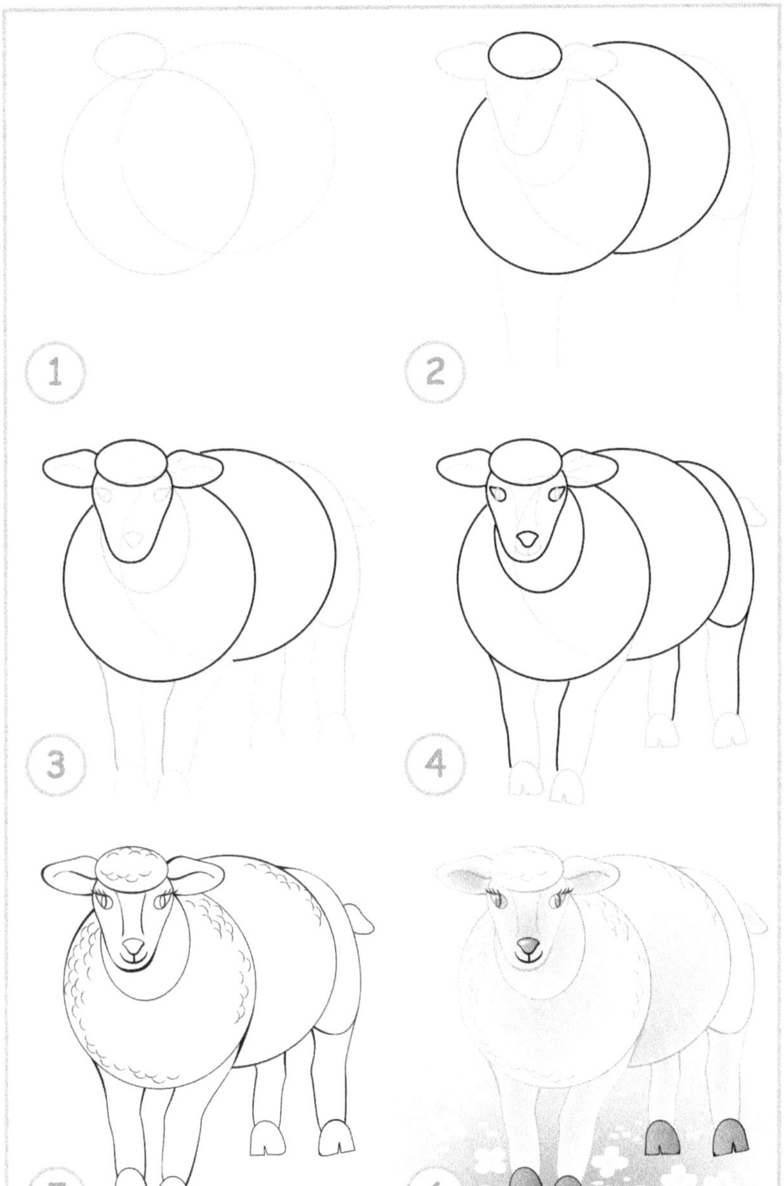
1
2
3
4
5
6

1
2
3
4
5
6

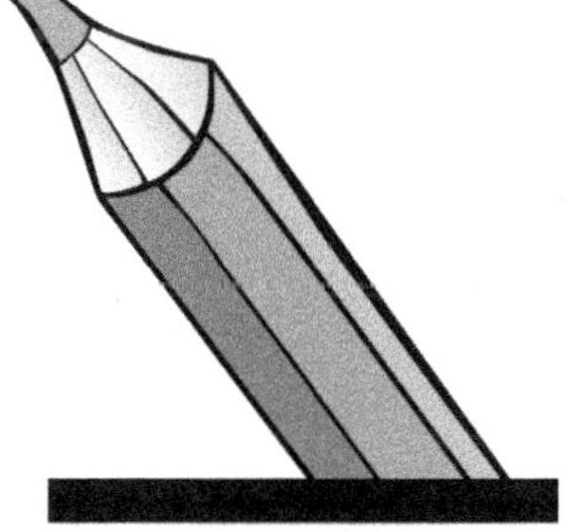

1
2
3
4
5
6

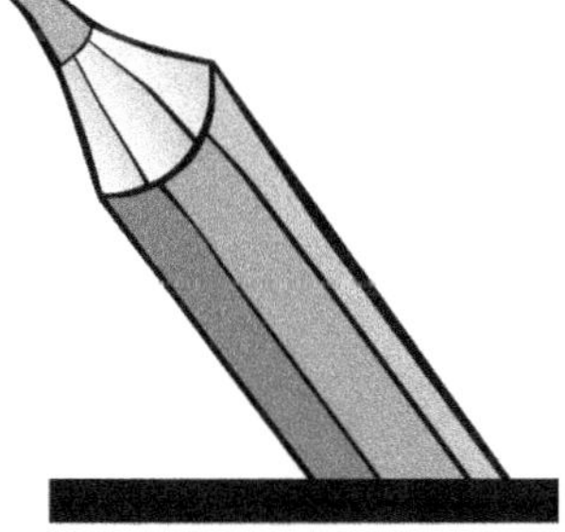

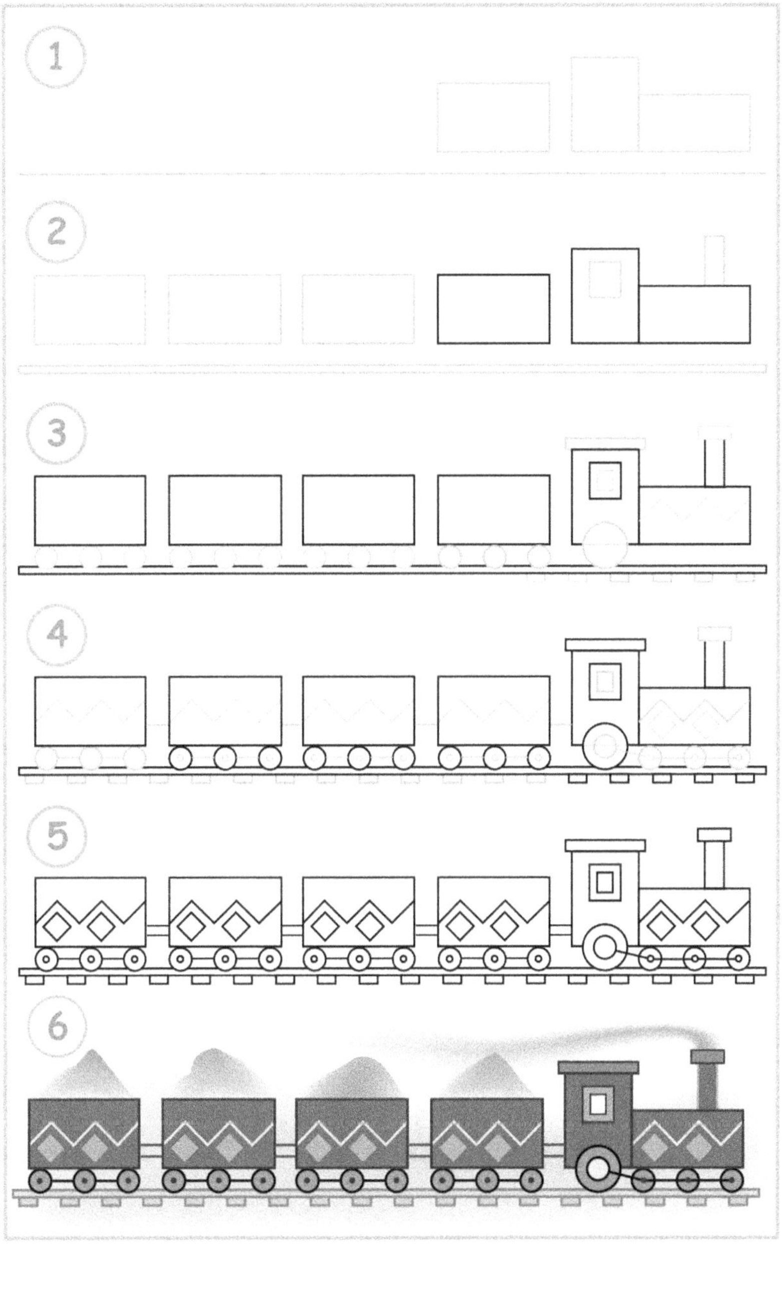
1
2
3
4
5
6

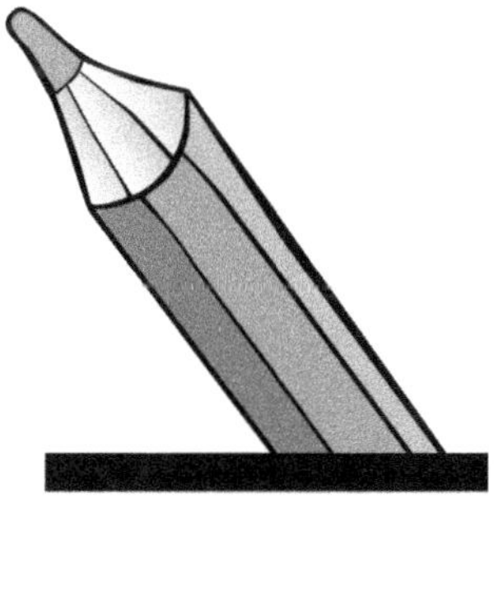

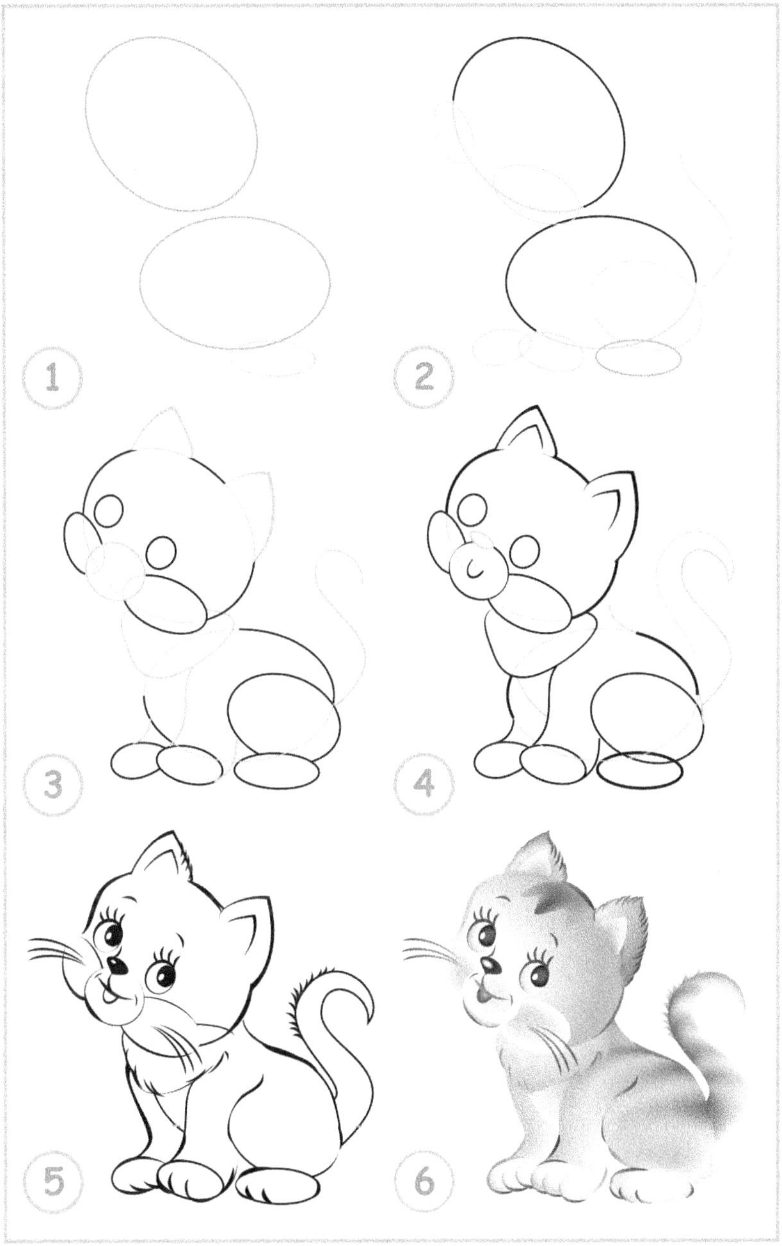
1
2
3
4
5
6

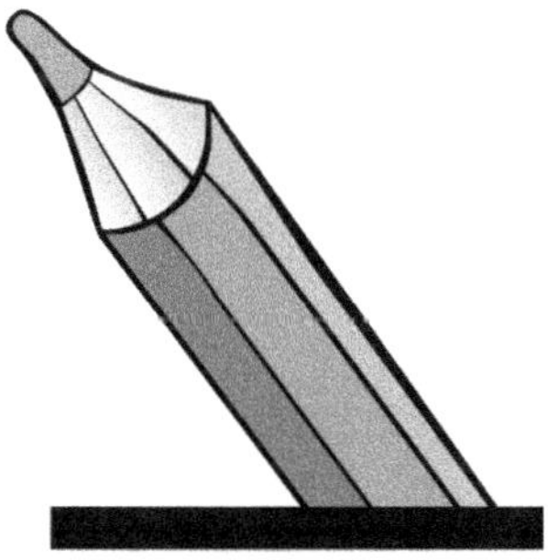

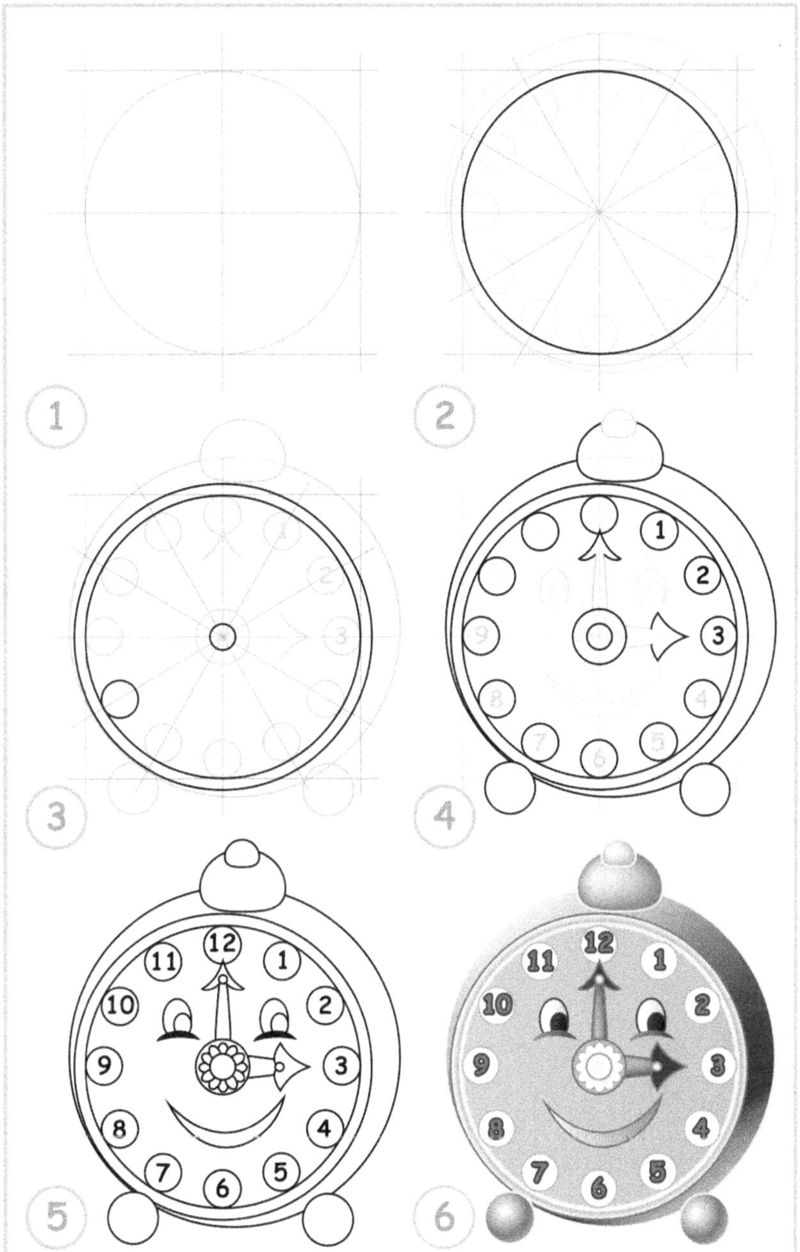
1
2
3
4
5
6

1
2
3
4
5
6

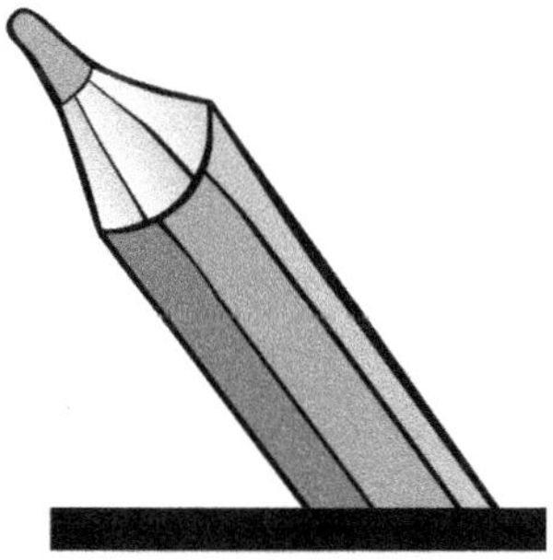

1
2
3
4
5
6

1
2
3
4
5
6

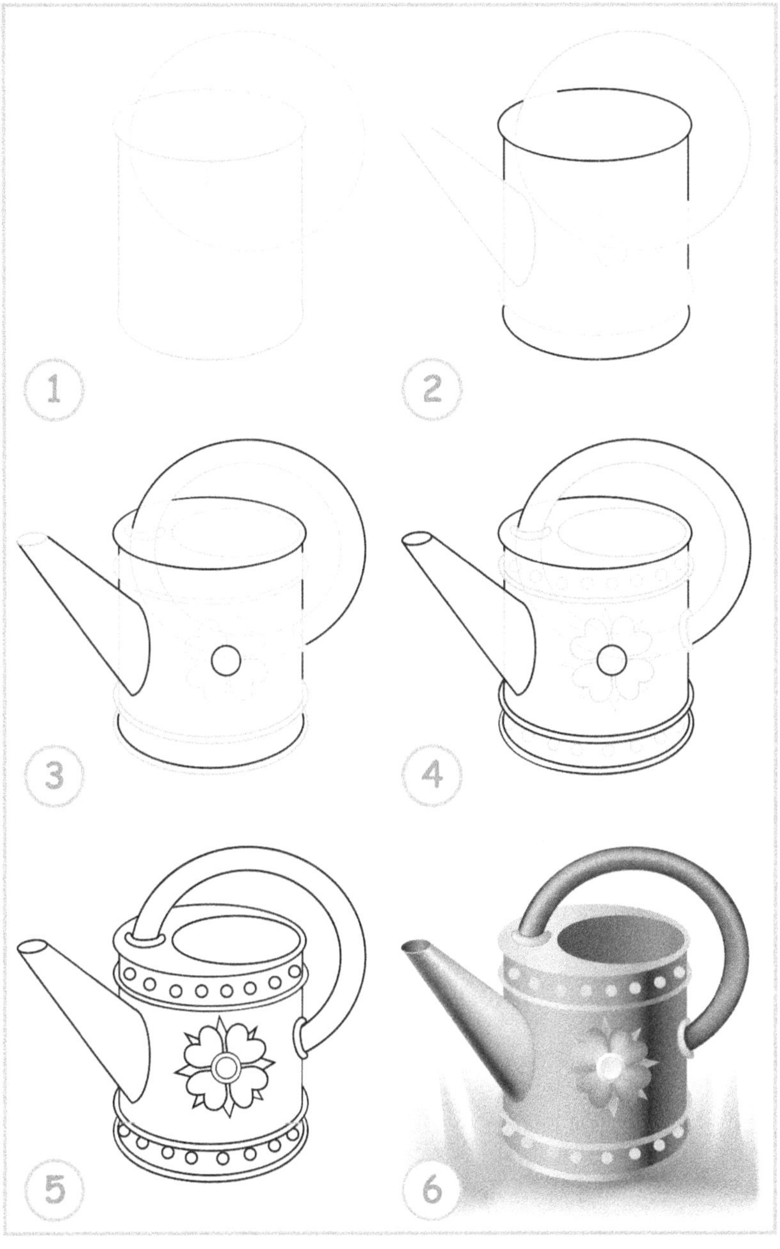
1
2
3
4
5
6

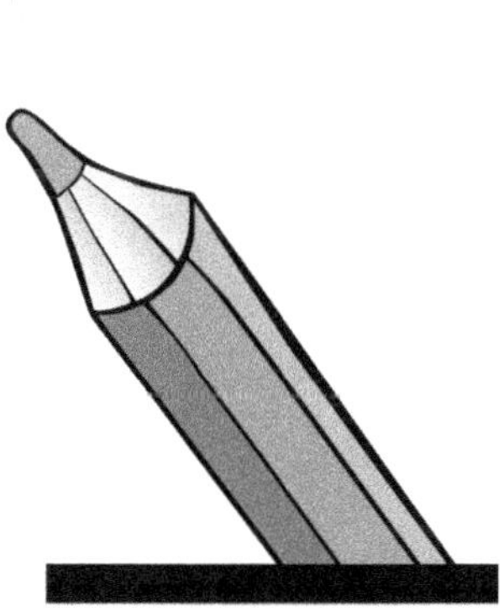

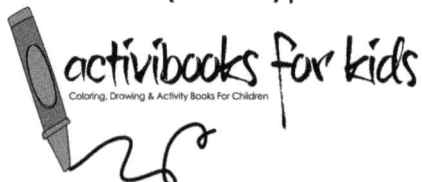

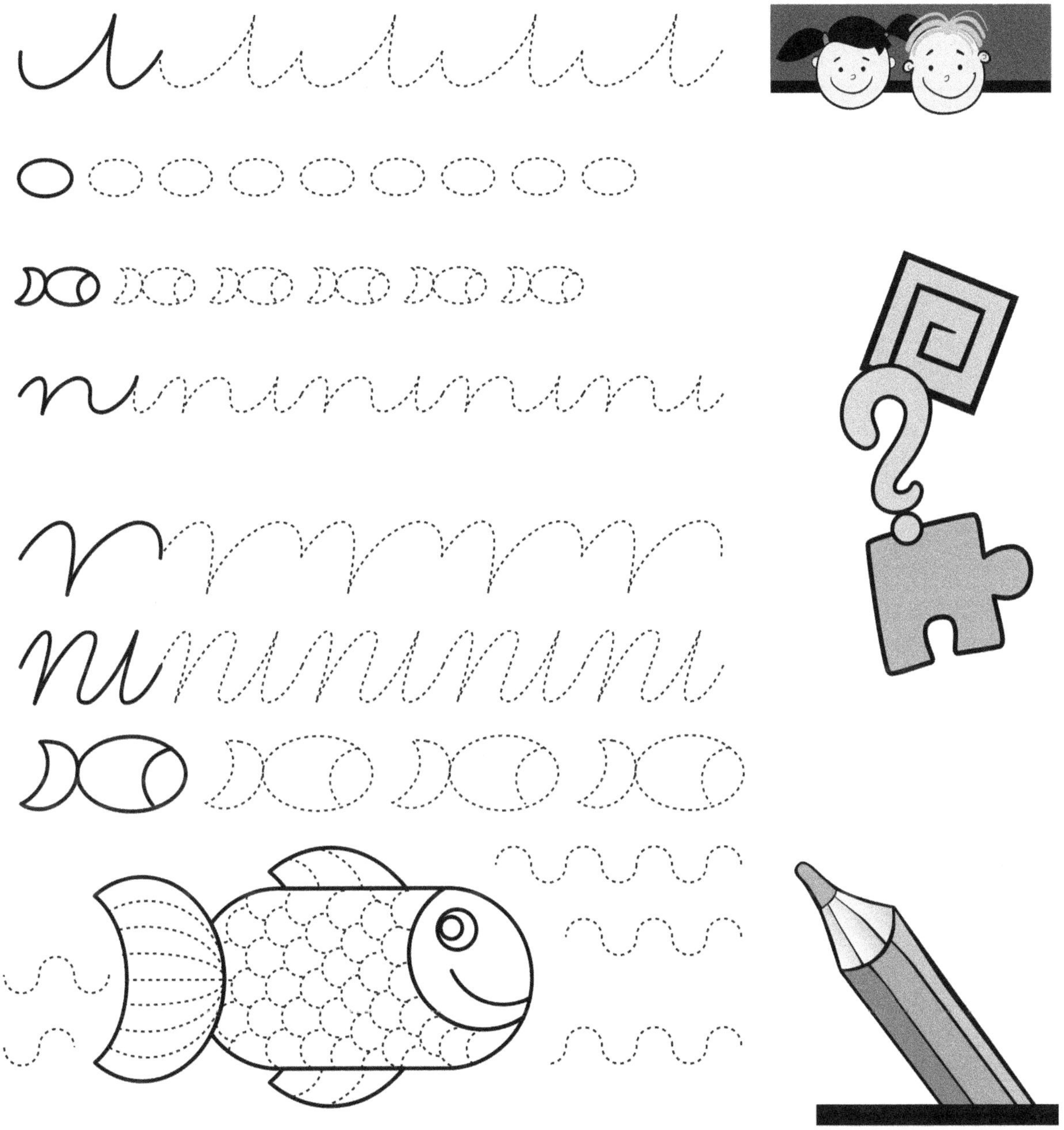

www.ingramcontent.com/pod-product-compliance
Lightning Source LLC
LaVergne TN
LVHW080249090426
835508LV00042BA/1509